CESAR CHAVEZ

by GINGER WADSWORTH
illustrations by MARK SCHRODER

On My Own
BIOGRAPHY

M Millbrook Press/Minneapolis

To those of you who supported the
United Farm Workers by not buying grapes.
—G. W.

The photograph on page 46 appears courtesy of © Bettman/CORBIS.

Quotation on p. 47: Richard Groswald del Castillo and Richard A. Garcia, *César Chávez: A Triumph of Spirit.* (Norman, OK: University of Oklahoma Press, 1995).

Text copyright © 2005 by Ginger Wadsworth
Illustrations copyright © 2005 by Mark Schroder

This book is available in two editions.
Library binding by Millbrook Press,
  a division of Lerner Publishing Group, Inc.
Soft cover by First Avenue Editions,
  an imprint of Lerner Publishing Group, Inc.
241 First Avenue North
Minneapolis, MN 55401 USA

For reading levels and more information, look up this title at www.lernerbooks.com.

Library of Congress Cataloging-in-Publication Data

Wadsworth, Ginger.
    Cesar Chavez / by Ginger Wadsworth.
        p.   cm. — (On my own biography)
    ISBN: 978-1-57505-652-4 (lib. bdg. : alk. paper)
    ISBN: 978-1-57505-826-9 (pbk. : alk. paper)
    ISBN: 978-1-57505-904-4 (EB pdf)
    1. Chavez, Cesar, 1927—Juvenile literature. 2. Labor leaders—United States—
Biography—Juvenile literature. 3. Mexican Americans—Biography—Juvenile
literature. 4. Mexican American agricultural laborers—History—Juvenile literature.
5. Agricultural laborers—Labor unions—United States—History—Juvenile literature.
I. Title. II. Series.
HD6509.C48W33 2005
331.88'13'092—dc22   2004006571

Manufactured in the United States of America
11 – CG – 11/1/15

Arizona

1933

When Cesario Chavez was six years old,
it was time for him to start school.
Cesario walked down the dusty road
to school with his big sister, Rita.
He was scared.
So he held Rita's hand.
Cesario's feet hurt.
He was not used to wearing shoes.

Cesario's teacher shortened his name
to "Cesar."

Cesar sounded less Mexican,
the teacher said.

The teacher told the children
to speak English.

Speaking English was hard.

Everyone spoke Spanish at home.

Many times, Cesar forgot to speak English.

Then the teacher hit his fingers with a ruler.

Cesar's grandparents had been born
in Mexico.

Cesar's grandfather had worked
for a cruel rancher.

The rancher whipped his workers.

Finally, Cesar's grandfather escaped
to Arizona.

He brought his family with him.

Cesar's father, Librado,
met Cesar's mother, Juana, in Arizona.

She had been born in Mexico too.

Cesar was born near Yuma, Arizona.
Richard and Lenny
were Cesar's little brothers.
Vicky was the baby.
They lived in a house
made of thick adobe bricks.
The house stayed cool in the summer
and warm in the winter.

At night, Cesar watched his father
make toy cars from tin cans
and small pieces of wood.
Cesar and his brothers played
with their cars on the floor.
At bedtime, their grandmother listened
to the children's prayers.

Everyone in the Chavez family worked
on their farm.
Cesar's father planted seeds in the dirt.
He hoed away the weeds.
He dug ditches to bring water
from the river to the farm.
Without water, the crops could not grow.

Cesar and Richard fed the horses, cows,
and chickens.

They gathered eggs.

Rita washed clothes by hand.

Juana made tortillas from ground corn.

Their family was poor.

But Juana still invited homeless people
to eat with them.

No one should go hungry, she believed.

Cesar's aunts, uncles, and cousins
lived nearby.
Sometimes they came to the Chavez farm
for fiestas.
Everyone ate a lot of good food.
Cesar and his cousins swam in the ditches.
They rode horses and climbed trees.
It was a good life.

Hard Times
1930s

In the 1930s,

millions of people lost their jobs.

Banks closed.

So did many stores.

Many people did not have enough money
to buy food.

They had to sell their homes and farms.

It was the Great Depression.

The Chavez family still had lots of milk,

eggs, and vegetables.

They had enough to sell and enough to eat.

Then there was a drought.

Without rain, the ditches dried up.

Without water,

the family could not grow crops.

There wasn't enough corn
for the chickens to eat.
So the chickens stopped laying eggs.
There wasn't enough grass
for the cows to eat.
So the cows stopped making milk.

In 1938, Cesar's family had to sell their land.

They drove to California to look for work.

Cesar was 11.

There were lots of big farms in California.

The farmers needed people
to plant and weed and pick the crops.

People traveled from farm to farm to work.

They were called migrant workers.

In the spring,
the Chavez family planted seeds.

It was cold in the fields.

Usually, Cesar was barefoot.

Shoes cost too much money.

It was hot work in the summer.
Cesar chopped weeds
with a short-handled hoe.
His back hurt.
It was hard to bend over all day.
Sometimes the fields smelled of poisons
called pesticides.
The farmers sprayed pesticides
to kill insects that might eat the plants.
Some of these pesticides
made the workers sick.

The children pulled oranges and lemons
from the trees.
They picked peas, beans, and cotton.
The workers filled boxes
with fruits and vegetables.
They were paid by the weight of each box.

Everyone in the family worked.

It was the only way they could earn
enough money.

If a family would not work for low pay,
there was always another family
to take its place.

When the crops were picked on one farm,
the Chavez family drove to another.

They needed the money.

The Chavez family stayed in farm camps
for migrant workers.
The farm camps were crowded and dirty.
The Chavez family squeezed into a shack.
It had a dirt floor and no bathroom.
When it rained, everything got wet.
There was lots of mud.

Many farm camps had tents, not shacks.

The tents were small.

Cesar and Richard had to sleep outside.

Rita slept in the car.

Juana cooked outside in a big metal can.

She still fed anyone who was hungry.

When they needed food, Cesar's parents
shopped in the nearest town.
Signs over some stores said
White Trade Only.
Cesar's family was Mexican.
They could not shop at those stores.

Cesar missed Arizona.

He wanted to ride a horse.

He wanted to climb a tree.

When his toy car was stolen,

Cesar wanted to hurt whoever took it.

Juana told her son not to fight.

It takes two to fight, she always said.

Fix your problems with words, she added.

Growing Up
1942

When he was 15, Cesar met

Helen Fabela in Delano, California.

Her parents were in Delano to pick cotton.

Cesar and Helen married in 1948.

Their first son, Fernando,

was born the next year.

More children soon followed.

Cesar and Helen worked hard.
They picked beans, strawberries,
and other crops.
They were each paid
about one dollar an hour.
It was not enough money
for food, clothes, or a simple house.
Cesar believed that migrant families
deserved better.

Cesar read books about leaders.

He wanted to learn

how they helped people improve their lives.

Then Cesar met Dolores Huerta.

She helped Mexican American

farmworkers.

He met Fred Ross.

Fred wanted the migrant workers

to become U.S. citizens.

Then they could vote.

They could vote for workers' rights.

Dolores and Fred had some good ideas.

They believed that people *together*

could make changes in their lives.

Even poor Mexican Americans *together*

had power.

Like his mother, Cesar wanted
to help other people.
So Cesar helped Mexican Americans
sign up to vote.
Cesar and Dolores started a union,
a group of workers.
It was the first union for farmworkers
in the United States.

Cesar traveled all over California.
He talked to workers in farm towns.
If they joined the union, he told them,
they would be a team.
They could ask the farm owners
for changes.
If the owners said no,
the union could go on strike.
All the people in the union would stop
working until the changes were made.

Many of the workers listened to Cesar.

He was a good leader.

Maybe he was right.

They were tired of living in a shack or tent.

They wanted clean water to drink.

They didn't want to work

near the pesticides that made them sick.

The changes would be hard to get,
they knew.
Cesar knew it too.
But he would try.
And he would do it peacefully.
Cesar did not believe in fighting
with his fists.

Many people thought that Cesar
would fail.

Rich families or big companies
owned most farms.

Cesar was poor.

He had dark skin.

And he was only a farmworker,
one of thousands.

Action!

1965

Cesar was becoming a strong union leader.
The union decided it was time to strike.
The workers would not pick grapes
in California.
Grapes rotted on the vines.
The farm owners lost money.

Cesar asked shoppers
to stop buying grapes.
Many families listened.
They did not buy grapes.
Some stores would not even sell grapes.
Many drivers would not carry grapes
in their trucks.
The farm owners lost more money.

The workers worried.

They weren't being paid.

How would they feed their families?

They would have to find work

picking other crops.

Cesar told them to be patient.

Workers have rights, he said.

A year passed.

It was time to tell more people
about the strike.

Cesar led a march of workers
to the capital city of California in 1966.

It took them 25 days to walk 300 miles
from Delano to Sacramento.

The word spread.

Workers from other states came
to walk with Cesar.

Actors, students, and government leaders
joined the marchers.

Along the way, other farmworkers
gave them food and water.

Cesar's feet hurt.

He had a high fever.

But he kept walking.

People read about the march
in newspapers.
They saw news about it on television.
Some people agreed
that migrant farmworkers should be helped.
Other people disagreed.
The grape strike continued.
In more and more states,
Americans stopped buying grapes.
Cesar and the union *were*
making a difference!

After five years, the owners
of the grape farms finally gave in.
The grape strike ended in 1970.
The workers got better pay.
They got some money for doctors.
Cesar was tired but happy.
It was a good start.
The farmworkers went back to work.

After the Strike
1970

Cesar and Helen lived simply.
They had eight children.
The union paid for their home and food.
Cesar had enough money
to support his family.

Every day, Cesar worked for the union.

He went to meetings.

He led new marches.

He gave speeches.

He wanted to make sure *all* farmworkers
were treated fairly.

Sometimes he was gone from home
for weeks.

He was always tired.

Cesar died one night in 1993.

His kind heart had worn out too soon.

He was only 66.

California's state flags were lowered

to half-mast to honor Cesar.

His brother Richard made him a pine coffin.

Cesar was buried near Delano.

About 40,000 people came to his funeral.

Most of them were migrant farmworkers.

All of his life, Cesar helped others.

He helped with words, not with his fists.

Cesar Chavez speaks at a rally on the twentieth anniversary of the first grape strike.

Afterword

Many honored Cesar Chavez for his work. In 1990, Mexico gave him the Aztec Eagle, that country's highest award. In 1994, the year after Cesar died, the Chavez family traveled to Washington, D.C. They accepted the Presidential Medal of Freedom at the White House in Cesar's memory.

Other leaders who believed in accomplishing change without violence had inspired Cesar. Mohandas Gandhi and Martin Luther King Jr. were two of those leaders. Cesar didn't think it was right to have a car, television, or other things until everyone in the world had basic human rights.

Cesar Chavez and Dolores Huerta started the National Farm Workers Association (NFWA) in 1962. It became the United Farm Workers of America (UFW). Many of Cesar's friends and several of his children continue to work for the UFW. Members of the UFW still march to Sacramento, California. They ask the state government for changes and laws that would help migrant workers. Marchers call out *"viva la causa,"* which means "long live the cause."

The state of California honors Cesar Chavez every March 31. It is the first such holiday for a Latino leader. Children read about Cesar. They celebrate his life. Schools, streets, and parks are named after him.

Millions of migrant farmworkers live in the United States. They earn low wages for hard, dangerous work. Migrant farmworkers get sick more easily than other U.S. workers do. Their children live in poverty. And too many of them get cancer. Doctors and public health workers worry about pesticides, the poisonous chemicals that are used in the fields.

Cesar Chavez dedicated his life to helping others, and his work must go on. As he said in 1968, "Our lives are all that really belong to us. So it is how we use our lives that determines what kind of men we are."

Important Dates

1927—Cesar Chavez was born on March 31 near Yuma, Arizona.

1937–44—Moved around California with his family as migrant farmworkers

1942—Finished eighth grade

1944—Joined the U.S. Navy

1948—Married Helen Fabela

1962—Started the National Farm Workers Association

1965—Grape pickers' strike began.

1966—Cesar led protest march to Sacramento.

1970—Grape growers gave in to the union. Cesar went to jail for refusing to call off lettuce strike.

1972—NFWA changed name to the United Farm Workers of America.

1975—State of California passed the Agricultural Labor Relations Act, the first bill of rights for farmworkers.

1988—Cesar protested against the use of pesticides.

1990—Awarded the Aguila Azteca (Aztec Eagle), Mexico's highest award

1991—Spoke to colleges throughout the United States

1993—Died on April 23 in Arizona

1994—Awarded the Presidential Medal of Freedom. His family started the Cesar E. Chavez Foundation.